Holiday4free.com

How to Swim
Easily and Enjoyably

A guide for parents and trainers

✔ Swimming rules for coloring
✔ Step-by-step motivation
✔ 3 exercises to practice at home
✔ 6 typical mistakes that parents should avoid
✔ Creative games (diving obstacle course & treasure hunt)
✔ Help with deep diving & jumping

The tips have been successfully applied and further developed with over 1,000 learners over a period of 10 years. Enjoy using this well-proven guide with descriptive photos for trainers, for beginner swimmers, for self-learners, to prepare and to accompany a swimming course.

Imprint

© Holiday4free.com
Christopher & Manuel Willer GbR
Paul-Jerchel-Str. 1, 14641 Nauen, Germany
Printer: see last page

ISBN Paperback: 978-3-947809-40-0
ISBN eBook Kindle: 978-3-947809-42-4

I0087937

Swimming rules for coloring

Do not go into the water
with a full stomach!

Avoid sunbathing for too long
and cool off before going
into the water!

Only go to the belly
or with parents in the water!

Don't jump into an
unknown body of water!

Beware of thunderstorms!
Get out of the water!

Be considerate of others!

Don't run when it's slick!
Never call for help for no reason!
Keep the water and the environment clean!

Don't go into the water if you're not feeling well!
Leave the water when you are cold!

Do not swim or dive where others jump into the water and do not jump where others practice swimming!

Do not swim far out hold your hands on the edge of the pool!
Floating aids can break!

Never swim where there are ships, dangerous waves or swirls!

Contents

Learn to Swim & Dive
for Children and Adults

We show 3 effective exercises to do at home and 6 common mistakes that parents should absolutely avoid if they want to teach their children how to swim themselves.

As our swim school receives so many applications that the waiting time is several years, we've decided to publish our experiences in an illustrated guide containing 15 professional tips, including tips drawn from practical experience.

Learning how to swim is a very important topic for all children and adults. With the right approach, swimming can be learned playfully and easily.

Foreword

Have you ever asked yourself how a swimming teacher manages, in just a few hours, to teach children something that parents have been trying to train their child in all summer?

Why is it that children also have so much fun with the swimming teacher and even want to practice more?

How come children happily dive and leap into the water after a few hours, even though some of them were extremely frightened of water when just washing their hair?

The key to success is a step-by-step, systematic approach. Unlike 'doggy paddling', the breaststroke technique is not a naturally inborn sequence of movements – so the intervals between the swimming lessons should not be too long. Developing this new, efficient movement takes time and patience, as it's made up of a number of individual movements.

Without proper guidance, particularly during the initial phase of getting used to the water, diving and breathing techniques, so many mistakes are made that the learner chokes on water, develops fears and loses interest. This is why it's a good idea to gain some professional knowledge beforehand, as this allows learning to swim to be an enjoyable experience, step by step.

Have fun with water sports

Experience the underwater world firsthand

Holiday4free.com

1. Personal motivation

A swimming teacher's recipe for success is to inspire instead of persuade. Both children and adults can be motivated by getting them to imagine the fascinating possibilities that arise once the element of water becomes safely accessible. From water sports with friends to seaside holidays and the underwater world at a dream beach…

A common mistake

Parents often try to push their children into swimming too early on. Just lovingly invite your child to learn if they like and then wait till they themselves freely develop the desire to swim. This makes learning easier, as well as much more effective in the long run.

Holiday4free.com

2.1. Awakening curiosity in the individual child

The swimming teacher will do their best to inspire the children so much beforehand, that they can hardly wait to finally get into the water.

Depending on what the learner likes doing best, they can be invited to learn in completely individual ways. A child that likes singing can be introduced with melodies, while a child who likes painting can be engaged with a colouring story for beginner swimmers. Always lead them gently and kindly from the familiar to the unfamiliar.

The picture shows the children being inspired to playfully engage with the topic as a group by colouring in the swimming rules.

Holiday4free.com

2.2. Bringing curiosity and anticipation to lessons

During the course, too, these stories can be a great accompaniment for beginner swimmers. The learners can already overcome their fears beforehand and treat the topic like a new, fun game. The playful aspect is important for creating a feeling of excited anticipation.

It's invaluable to attune to the unique interests and inclinations of each child. There may be a water game that sparks a child's sense of wonder or a story that deeply engages them. What's crucial is ensuring that children remain passionate, always eager for their subsequent aquatic adventure.

3. The perfect preparation

The surrounding conditions are a decisive factor. Learning to swim works best in as undisturbed an environment as possible. When very few people are in the water and the noise level is low, a learner can concentrate best and learn fast. It's extremely important for the water to be clear, clean and warm to give the learner has a sense of well-being at all times.

A common mistake

Parents try to teach their children swimming anywhere. Slides, waves and whirlpools make concentrated learning more difficult. Overcrowded water parks filled with other splashing, romping children distract the learner. The murky, dark waters of a lake, where they can't see the bottom, can make the learner feel even more insecure.

Holiday4free.com

4. Gaining trust step by step

It is important for the learner to be able to trust their teacher completely. Give them a lot of time to get used to the water and practice in chest-high water until they gain the confidence to go further. A calm voice, eye contact and supportive touches will give them a sense of safety.

A common mistake

If the teacher promises not to let go of the learner or to catch them when they jump into the water, then they must keep that promise, even if it means that learning takes a bit longer. Honoring such promises strengthens the foundation of trust between the teacher and the learner..

Holiday4free.com

5. A swimming teacher needs the patience of a saint

It sometimes helps to take the learner's hand and give them more time. It often makes sense to simply continue practicing next time. However, the intervals between swimming lessons should not be too long, as regular – preferably daily – training is needed to make progress. The swimming teacher should ensure that the challenge is appropriate. They should include breaks and variety during the swimming lesson if the learner needs to gather new strength or still needs some time for the next step. Both phases – effort and relaxation – are equally important.

A common mistake

Most parents are so delighted that their child finally feels like learning to swim that they overdo the time spent in the water. Give them space to really look forward to their next swimming lesson and start by celebrating the small achievements.

Holiday4free.com

6. Building self-confidence

An affectionate word, a smile, having fun together and praise (even for small achievements) helps to build self-confidence and encourages the learner to take on bigger challenges.

There's always something worth praising, as every child has special talents that need to be discovered, acknowledged and valued.

A common mistake

The breaststroke technique is very complex because of the need to coordinate many sub-movements and should not be taught too soon – otherwise, particularly in the case of younger learners, this can detract from their self-confidence. You can already start getting a child used to the water and to moving forward through the water naturally before the age of 5.

Holiday4free.com

7. That fine difference

When several children are learning to swim together, it's important for the teacher to be able to differentiate between them. Each learner brings different prior experiences and requirements to the course and should be praised individually for their achievements.

While it may be an achievement for one child to jump into the water and to swim the whole length of the pool, it is a huge achievement for another child to work up the courage to duck their head under the water. Both achievements are valuable in their own way.

Learners shouldn't compare themselves with others, but should instead feel happy about their own strengths, gifts and steps on the path to success, and build on those.

Holiday4free.com

8. Important basic skills and moving forward through the water naturally

A swimming teacher needs to work on the basics very thoroughly before even starting with the actual swimming movement. Feeling comfortable in the water and mastering basic skills are very important for taking the next steps. These include, for example, gliding, floating, breathing, diving, moving forward through the water naturally and feeling comfortable on one's back in the water.

At first, the children should be allowed to move through the water in a natural way, before being taught the proper technique for the breaststroke. To start with, the doggy paddle, backstroke, and initial crawling strokes allow them to move through the water before being able to actually swim.

9.1. Learning to swim with the eyes and the right arm movement

People take in most information through their eyes, so this is the easiest way to learn something new.

"It is easy to observe the arm movement with the eyes. Here, it is important to make sure that the hands and shoulders are under water. When pushing back the water, the wrists should be stable, the thumbs should point downwards and the fingers should be together. When the legs are pushing the body forward, the arms should be stretched straight out in front, to enable the body to glide through the water more easily and optimal use of the strength of the legs for forward motion. This rhythm enables energy-saving swimming movements."

When doing the breaststroke, the legs are not in the learner's field of vision and they can't consciously follow the leg movements with their eyes.

9.2. Consciously practicing, automate and the right leg movement

In practice, it has proved effective to initially shift the leg movement to the front, within the learner's field of vision, and to practice it without water at first.

This allows the eyes to consciously observe the movements of the legs and small technical mistakes to be put right by the learner themselves.

This makes it easier to learn the leg movement, which gives the learner an experience of success and motivates them.

An exercise to do at home

The legwork exercise is suitable for practicing in the sand, or at home on a smooth floor. The learner sits down and practices doing the frog movement with their legs:

"Slowly draw the legs up, then open and straighten them with a powerful push away from the body and bring them together stretched out to the front. When opening the legs, the knees should point outwards and the tips of the toes should point upwards."

This new movement can learned be more attentively and consciously on land, as in the water most of a learner's concentration is needed to orient themselves, to maintain their balance and to keep their airways free. Once the learner has internalized the sequence of movements, they can continue practicing in the water.

When making the first attempts in the water, it makes sense to practice the legwork while on one's back in the water. The learner's buoyancy can be supported using a floatation aid or a helping hand from the teacher. In this way, the learner can also see their own legwork in the water and improve it themselves. As soon as that movement has become automatic, the learner can go on to practice in the breast position. This method makes it easier to move the legs correctly in the breast position, even when they are outside the learner's field of vision.

Extra tip from practical experience

Children quickly become bored if they have to do the exercise alone. Try to arrange for them to do the dry exercise together with another child, to a song or melody. You can also count the number of movements by counting down from 10 to 0 in a different language. The child should learn to do the correct movements automatically over many days.

Holiday4free.com

10. Learning to swim with the ears

When teaching beginners to swim, communication in the water should differ from that on land. The noise level and acoustics in swimming pools are quite intense. Furthermore, learners often swim with their heads submerged, which means that the teacher's well-intentioned instructions can go unheard if the student's ears are underwater.

Hearing and understanding in water

Pools are a symphony of sounds: the splashing of water, conversations of swimmers and spectators, and the hum of ventilation systems. Amidst this cacophony, delivering clear instructions can be challenging. Therefore, it's crucial that communication between the teacher and learner is well-coordinated, especially for beginners and children to feel comfortable.

The teacher's role

Teachers need to exhibit empathy and patience. They should hold off on giving explanations until after the exercise is complete, ensuring the student's ears are free from water.

Every learner has their unique way of understanding; while some benefit from visual demonstrations, others might prefer precise verbal instructions.

Non-verbal cues, such as a reassuring nod or a thumbs-up, can significantly boost a beginner's motivation and self-confidence. Such gestures can assure the learner they're on the right track and encourage them to persist. Establishing a bond of trust between teacher and learner is invaluable, and such simple signs can greatly facilitate this.

Combining visual and verbal communication

Should a teacher wish to provide guidance during a swimming exercise, they must remain in the student's line of sight and demonstrate any movements as soon as the student is receptive. Effective communication in the water requires a different approach than on land. For instance, divers exclusively use hand signals and gestures underwater. A combination of both methods proves most effective.

A common mistake

It's not uncommon for teachers to shout instructions from outside the student's visual field. However, this approach is discouraged. During such moments, the learner's entire focus is on executing movements, which they're performing with great effort just to stay afloat.

Holiday4free.com

11. From blowing to diving

Non-swimmers should be introduced to the water gently and kindly. This begins with blowing. When the learner blows out hard, pressure arises in the nasal and oral cavities. The outflowing air prevents water from getting into the nose. The blowing should already start underwater, before resurfacing.

After blowing away the remaining droplets, the learner can inhale without coughing. This sets a vital foundation for future jumps and dives without needing to pinch the nose.

By blowing in the water, we learn to control our breathing and understand the rhythm of inhalation and exhalation better. This not only builds confidence in the water but also deepens our understanding of our own body.

The value of playful learning

It's amazing how many skills we can acquire through play. When it comes to blowing and diving, it's about learning technical skills as well as developing a joy and curiosity for the water. Through playful exercises, like blowing out candles or playing with soap bubbles, learning becomes a fun and rewarding experience.

The joy of diving

Once the basics of blowing are understood, a whole new world opens up beneath the water's surface. Diving becomes an adventure where the wonders of underwater life can be discovered. Whether it's about collecting items from the pool floor or simply enjoying the serene world beneath the water's surface, diving offers countless opportunities for fun and exploration.

An exercise to do at home

Blowing can be practiced at home by simply pouring some clean water into a bowl, washbasin, or the bathtub and then blowing hard into it. Children who like playing at blowing bubbles can practice blowing with long, even breaths. Blowing in powerful, explosive puffs can be practiced when blowing out candles.

Even if this breathing exercise may seem funny to adult learners, it makes sense in adult swimming too, in order to start trusting the water and to learn to swim safely later on.

12.1. Preparation for diving

To begin with, the breathing technique is trained on land or in shallow water, to prevent anyone later choking on water during their first swimming attempts. Everyone accidentally "goes under" now and again when they first start learning to swim. To prevent the learner experiencing this as unpleasant or even panicking, the swimming teacher should take a lot of time beforehand to present diving as an enjoyable game.

An exercise to do at home

Diving can be practiced at home by first trying to hold the breath out of the water for as long as possible and then blowing hard again. Anyone who can hold their breath for 3 seconds can also try doing it with their head under water. After that, the time can be increased step by step.

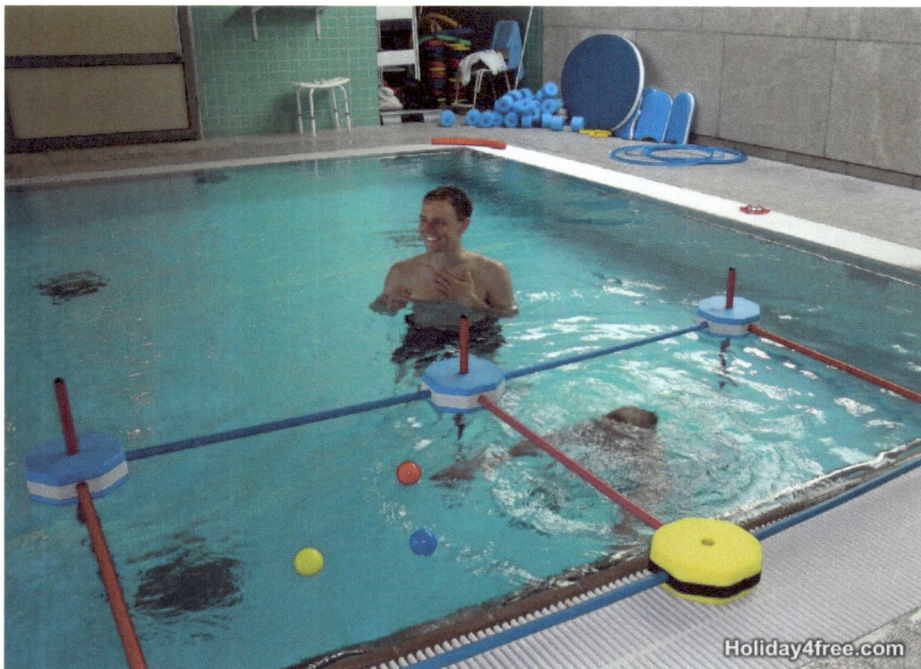

Holiday4free.com

12.2. The diving obstacle course
and the initial successes

The diving obstacle course is fun and is a valuable teaching aid. During their first diving attempts, some swimming learners don't yet feel confident enough to duck their whole head under water. The colourful bar of the diving obstacle course floats on the surface of the water and invites learners to dive. This playful approach encourages them to dive under the bar.

This gives the learner the inner motivation to duck their whole head under water to overcome this obstacle in the game. After the learner has managed simple exercises, the obstacle course can be extended and creative accessories like water balls can be used.

Holiday4free.com

12.3. Practicing deep diving

Deep diving is very important, because once the learner can dive to the bottom everywhere in the pool by themselves, they acquire a sense of familiarity and ease.

Diving into the depths poses a challenge for many learners, because they have to return to the surface of the water in order to breathe. In addition, they are not yet used to the water pressure deeper down, so it makes sense to support them on their way down with a climbing pole. The pole offers a sense of safety and orientation. Experience shows that it's possible to achieve great results using this simple method and that each learner can decide for themselves how deep they want to dive.

If pressure arises in the ears, it can be equalized as in a plane (by moving the jaw, tilting the head, swallowing or breathing into the nose while holding it closed).

Holiday4free.com

13.1. Orientation under water
is vitally important

Anyone who wants to be safe in the water should get used to diving with their eyes open and take enough time to practice this. A swimming teacher uses creative underwater games and invests many hours in training the ability to see under water.

Games in which 2 people look at one another under water, give signs, guess numbers or colours are suitable for doing this. Children like looking for things in water, doing a roll under water and diving through obstacles.

These exercises are an important basis for safety later on. After accidentally falling into water, being able to orient oneself under water is vitally important.

13.2. Using creative diving toys

Colourful, cute, funny diving toys can stimulate children's imagination. Practical experience shows that they make the first diving exercises a specially enjoyable underwater experience.

The children's imaginative power can be used to develop enjoyment and endurance. It makes a big difference whether the children are always having to dive for the same ring or have the exciting experience of finding colourful fish under water.

After many diving attempts, the eyes get used to seeing under water. Thanks to the creative diving toys, the children's enthusiasm for practicing lasts considerably longer, resulting in greater long-term safety in the water.

Holiday4free.com

13.3. The art of taking small steps

When learning to swim and dive, it makes sense to systematically build the exercises on top of one another, step by step. For example, pool steps are ideal for placing a diving object one step lower each time. This enable the learner to celebrate their achievements step by step and also to go back up a step to build up their courage again.

Later on, the diving toys can be set out in patterns on the pool bottom. The diving exercise can begin with all the toys simply lying in a row. The exercise can be made more challenging by setting out the objects in a zigzag and finally in triangles or rectangles.

Children love to choose the patterns themselves or to hide a diving toy in the water for another child.

Holiday4free.com

13.4. A treasure hunt in the water

With a bit of creativity, it's even possible to hold a treasure hunt in the water.

A waterproof treasure map and a message in a (glass-free) bottle can be used. Children who have a very special experience in the water will associate this positive experience with the water. This is extremely valuable and helpful in all further exercises. During the treasure hunt, the learners can already solve different riddles in the water and find clues under water. Laminated photographs of fish can be found in an adventurous search under the water.

This treasure hunt is great fun, which automatically ensures that the children will be even more enthusiastic about diving.

Holiday4free.com

14.1. Slowly reducing floatation aids

A safe and simple option for learning to swim is gradually cutting down on floatation aids.

With this method, many parents can even teach their children to swim themselves. As long as their technique is correct and the learner is strong enough, swim disks or cork floats can be removed little by little. With a little patience, the child will soon be able to swim without any floatation aids.

Two things can be observed here. On the one hand, floatation aids come in different designs and it is important to ensure that they are firmly fixed and can't come apart or slip off by themselves – while on the other, the number of swim corks and disks, or the air in the swimming pillow should be varied slightly.

Holiday4free.com

14.2. Training the arms and legs separately

The swimming teacher always takes exercises from easy to hard and from single to combined, step by step. It is easier if the movements of the arms and legs are first learned separately and later combined into a whole movement.

The learner needs to focus their whole concentration on their legwork as, in the breaststroke technique, this is made up of several elements.

To do this, the arms can be placed on a pool noodle or on a swimboard (a swimming aid), so that the learner can focus their whole attention on their legwork.

Using a rescue bar offers a further option for practicing the movements separately. The learner can hold onto this bar and specifically train their legs or push the water back with one arm, while the teacher pulls them through the water using the bar or a similar aid.

These exercises offer the possibility of training the arms and legs individually. Once the learner is able to carry out both partial movements independently of one another, their arm and leg movements can then be coordinated with one another.

Learners can initially be trained to move forward through the water by themselves in the shallows, or together with the teacher at the edge of the pool. Diving and orientation under water should be practiced thoroughly beforehand, to enable the learner to focus their whole attention on the sequence of movements. This makes it possible to carry out all movements calmly and carefully, even without a floatation aid.

If the head is laid down in the water during the first swimming attempts, the legs automatically float upwards. This results in a better water position and less resistance from the water. The whole body floats and relaxes. The focus here is on moving forwards under water. The water is pushed from front to back using the arms and the body is thereby stretched lengthwise. This enables a first easy forward movement through the water and motivates the learner to continue. This exercise thereby helps them to glide easily through the water and to have the first experiences of success.

Regular training helps the movements to become steadily stronger, almost automatically. As soon as a learner has developed enough strength and can perform the swimming technique correctly, they can direct their gaze upwards. This small change in their line of vision marks the beginning of swimming without aids.

Holiday4free.com

15. The brave jump

The jump is a "reward flight" for learning to swim. Some children find it easy to jump, while other children need a little support. To encourage them, the swimming teacher can take hold of both the learner's arms for the first jumps and make sure that their head doesn't go under.

Beginners also need to first develop a sense of safety and trust when jumping. The next step is to slowly let go of one hand and the head can be allowed to sink a little deeper under the water each time as the jumps progress.

To begin with, a child who doesn't feel confident enough to do this can also slip into the water from a sitting or squatting position at the pool edge. Once they have managed several jumps with assistance, the child can jump into the water completely alone.

Extra tip from practical experience

Many parents stand at the edge of the pool for a long time, trying to talk their child into jumping. The longer the child stands there, the harder it is for them to decide to do it.

After blowing and diving have been practiced thoroughly, the learner can be taken by the hand to inspire trust. A technique that has proved effective is to simply count up to 3 and to then gently let the child sink into the water up to their stomach. After each jump, the child can be encouraged with a good helping of praise.

Adult learners can squat down at the pool edge, hold onto the edge and then slowly jump into the water. This exercise should be repeated until they have built up a strong enough sense of safety: because when you trust the water, diving is really enjoyable.

After the first jumps have been managed safely, different jumping techniques can be tried out. It is important to be able to jump in many different ways, as every jumping technique has special advantages and areas of application. Those who prefer to jump into the water without diving deep can use the step jump or "package jump". As the legs are drawn up and embraced by the arms, the package jump is particularly safe. A racing dive helps the swimmer to go far and shallow, while the header dive is useful for gliding deep into the water with momentum and being able to pick up objects from the pool bottom. The header dive and the feet-first jump are great for diving or jumping from the diving platform.

Later on, the range of dives and jumps can be expanded. It's great fun to dive into water with a backflip, a roll or a corkscrew dive. Learning these different dives also teaches safety and playfully trains learners to cope with accidentally falling into water. Swimmers should never dive where others are diving or in unfamiliar waters.

Holiday4free.com

Additional tip:
Enjoying the water

It's important to implement all the tips step by step, until the learner has a safe grasp of the basics and can have fun in the water.

The feeling of happiness about their own progress creates inner motivation and makes them feel like spending more hours in the water. Thanks to regularly swimming and playing in the water, the learner's movements get steadily stronger and the distances they swim automatically get longer.

The different exercises, such as learning breathing techniques, water position, floating, gliding, diving, jumping, balancing and orientation ensure all-round safety in the water.

Holiday4free.com

Additional tip:
Recognizing and fostering talents

By paying a little attention, it's possible to discern individual talents and interests. Exercises which at first sight have nothing to do with a typical swimming lesson can create lasting enthusiasm for swimming and diving. With a bit of imagination and inventiveness, the tasks can be skilfully adapted.

Depending on a child's talents and interests, both musical and sporting aspects can be combined with the swimming exercises. You can use melodies, water balls and mermaid fins.

For example, working with a surfboard trains balance and teaches the fun of being in the element of water.

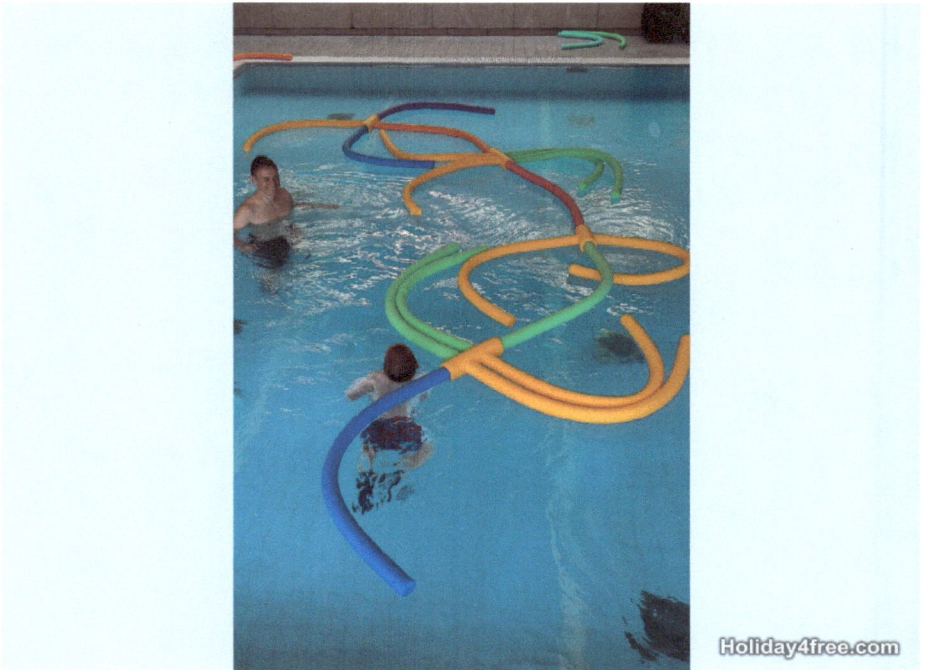

Additional tip:
Creativity inspires

Children who experience a treasure hunt in the water or manage to swim past an obstacle that they've built themselves can easily and happily swim considerable distances. At the same time, they develop endurance and strength.

"Achieving aims with fun and games"

Many years' experience has shown that children are much more venturesome when playing and that every swimming lesson can become a small adventure.

Creative diving toys and pool noodle connectors are ideal for making swimming lessons more creative.

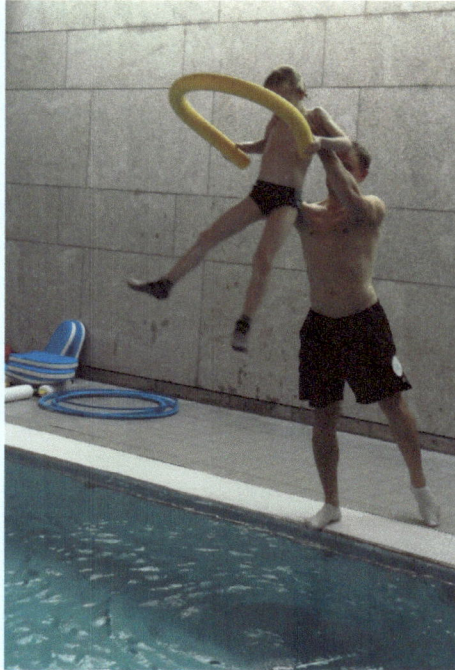

Additional tip:
Seeing through the learners' eyes

One of the most important recipes for success for a swimming teacher is still being able to see the world through the eyes of the children.

A swimboard placed on the surface of the water can represent the fin of a dolphin in the water or a swimming noodle can be a parachute on a flight into the water. Objects under water can create an exciting diving experience.

Thanks to these ingenious games, learners will gain a lasting enthusiasm for the element of water.

Holiday4free.com

Tips for parents about the swimming badges

A swimming badge is something very special. We congratulate all children who have achieved a badge and rejoice with them.

A "swim certificate" is a nice motivation on the way to becoming a safe swimmer.

Please keep in mind that just because the requirements of a swimming badge have been met, it doesn't necessarily mean your child can swim safely. This notice is also often printed on the back of the swim certificate. The badge on the swimming trunks does not automatically mean that a child will behave and perform properly in a real everyday or dangerous situation. A test is usually conducted under optimal conditions with clear, calm water, in a swimming pool.

In addition to the surprise effect, the water in a dangerous situation is usually not as calm as when tested in a familiar swimming pool. The child may even have long clothes and shoes on when they fall into the water.

Regular training is necessary for a child to be able to swim a distance of 25 meters after a surprise fall from the dock or boat.

More and more swim schools are offering advanced courses for developing safe swimmers. An advanced course is playful safety training that builds on the knowledge of the badge and equips swimmers with sustainable skills for real-life situations. Here, the overview, dodging, falling, self-rescue, personal responsibility, passive swimming with and without waves, and swimming with long clothing are trained.

For further information please visit:

www.Holiday4free.com

www.ingramcontent.com/pod-product-compliance
Lightning Source LLC
Chambersburg PA
CBHW040346060426
42445CB00029B/13